DIVINE BLESSINGS

PATH TOWARDS GOD

INAB RANI LOLU

In the name of God

The Most Gracious and The Most Merciful

Contents

Foreword

In the name of Allah whose affection and love allowed for the publication of the book. Salutations to the Prophet (sallalahu alyhi wasalam) whose tender mercy has shown me how to walk on faith. My parents fervent prayers, which altered the direction of my fate, are gently appreciated.

I dedicate this book to you all and to all the seekers who are lost and cannot find their way, to all the people who are not able to find mercy with the most Merciful.

Please do not give me credit if anything in this book inspires you to accomplish something in your life. Please understand that I am human, therefore please excuse my errors you may find in my lines.

I am writing this book to remind you that no matter how sad you are, how many sins you have committed in your past (knowingly or unknowingly), know that His mercy is limitless. He is Ar-Rahman (the most merciful).He loves you unconditionally no matter who you are. Place your trust in Him and let Him lead you back into the embrace of His everlasting love.

In order to make it clear to the English speaking reader that God and Allah are the same, I have used both terms interchangeably throughout this book. Despite the fact that the Arabic word for Allah i.e., God has many meanings that the English term God does not, it was thought necessary to utilise both words.

I am glad you found this book and my sincere hope is that you will discover buried parts of yourself in its pages. You must keep in mind that you contain the unfathomable and eternal breath of God and that cannot be taken away.

CHAPTER ONE

THE MERCY OF GOD

Most of the times, life turns out to be a complete mess. We are always in search of something that could be relaxing to our body and soothing to our soul. At times, we cry a lot but could not find anyone to make us feel better. We are in search of worldly pleasure. We roam here and there in search of peace. We turn out to people but everyone abandons us. For years, the same procedure continues. We rush out to people for mental peace but they destroy it. However, at times, we turn out to God but for a short span of time but again, we get distracted.

I was born Muslim but growing up, I was never taught how to love and be loved by God. I was taught how to offer prayers form the very beginning. I even went to a local Darasgah (kind of school meant for Islamic education) to learn Quran and related things. After some years, I left the Darasgah due to the burden of worldly education. However, i remained in touch with the Islamic procedures like offering prayers, reciting Qur'an etc. My parents (especially my mother) focussed on the knowledge of both the worlds i.e., this world and the hereafter.

When i grew up, i felt like I hardly know anything about Islam. I kept turning to God and saying, "I cannot do this task and I am not worthy of it". More often, I kept feeling unworthy of myself. However, I remained constant with my prayers and hardly skipped one. But somewhere deep in my heart, I felt like something was lagging behind. Then, I realized that the solutions to our most perplexing questions start to emerge when we allow the light of God to shine into the depths of our hearts.

Allah is the creator of the Universe, the One whose love encompasses all hearts, whose kindness and mercy encompasses all things and He is everywhere you look. God beckons us to turn to Him so that we may grow through Him. God is the One who can speak the death out of their graves and who can work miracles in seemingly hopeless situations. He is the One who turns hardships into victories and who turns the sufferer into a winner. God is present with us at all the times - both the beginning and the end. While we may take time to repent, god is abounding in mercy, charity, forgiveness and grace. God does not require our worship. We worship Him because we depend on Him. The hidden fruits of love that God plants within our spirit can only be reaped when our hearts yield to the light. As the Qur'an says, "WHOEVER ENDEAVOURS, STRIVES ONLY FOR HIS OWN SOUL BECAUSE ALLAH IS UTTERLY INDEPENDENT OF ALL WORLDS" (29:06). No matter how far we wander from God, all it takes is one thought to bring us back.

He is only One and we forget Him. On the other hand, he has billions of creatures but He never forgets a single one of us. His love is unconditional. We break our promises every time but remember that He is always faithful. We can only get relieved of our anxiety and fear when we get to know how much God loves us.

Allah is the bestower of mercy. He is the most merciful (Ar - Rahman) and the bestower of mercy (Ar - Rahim). So whenever we commit a sin, we should turn to Him. We should never give up in His mercy. We should ask Allah to pardon us if we make a mistake or if we are flawed and we should hope that He will pardon us. We are aware of His limitless mercy.

Ultimately, everyone has the choice to accept their blessings and use them as Allah has directed and worship Him alone.

"IF YOU WERE TO TRY AND COUNT THE FAVOURS OF ALLAH, YOU COULD NOT ENUMERATE THEM. INDEED, ALLAH IS MERCIFUL AND FORGIVING (Qur'an 16:18)"

Man was not left to confront the challenges of life on his own from the moment of his creation. God's mercy allowed man to receive revelation through prophets, who then taught it to their people in order to lead and safeguard them. Muhammad(sallallahu alahy wasalam) was the last of the prophets and the recipient of Qur'an which is the most perfect and merciful of all revelations. Qur'an is the world's greatest source of mercy and direction. In the same way that God sent messengers in the past, He also sent a living, flawless and useful example to show mankind how to put the Qur'anic teachings on mercy and justice into practise in our daily lives.

"AND GOD HAS NOT SENT YOU (MUHAMMAD) EXCEPT AS A MERCY FOR MANKIND" (Qur'an 21:107)

The creation of human beings with all their facilities is a huge mercy in itself. We should be thankful for the ability to wake up, go to work, eat, play and sleep every day.

"AND OUT OF HIS MERCY HE MADE FOR YOU THE NIGHT AND THE DAY THAT YOU MAY REST THEREIN AND (BY DAY) SEEK FROM HIS BOUNTY AND PERHAPS YOU WILL BE GRATEFUL" (Qur'an 28:73)

Another manifestation of Allah's mercy is His forgiveness of sins since He is aware of our flaws and shortcomings. The fact that believers sin does not indicate that we should give up on Allah's mercy or that His forgiveness is no longer available to us.

"O MY SERVANTS WHO HAVE TRANSGRESSED AGAINST THEIR SOULS! DO NOT DESPAIR OF THE MERCY OF GOD: FOR HE FORGIVES ALL SINS : FOR HE IS THE MOST FORGIVING AND MOST MERCIFUL" (Qur'an 39:53)

The attribute of justice co-exists with Allah's attribute of mercy.

"VERILY, FOR THE RIGHTEOUS, ARE GARDENS OF DELIGHT, IN THE PRESENCE OF THEIR LORD. SHALL WE THEN TREAT THE PEOPLE OF FAITH LIKE THOSE WHO DONNOT BELIEVE? WHAT IS THE MATTER WITH YOU ? HOW DO YOU JUDGE ?" (Qur'an 68:34-36)

Although Allah is the most Generous, He is also swift in reckoning. By repeatedly committing the same sins without real repentance or making the commitment to never return to the sin again, one cannot attempt to trick Allah and take advantage of His mercy.

"AND OF NO USE IN THE REPENTANCE OF THOSE WHO CONTINUE TO COMMIT SINS UNTIL DEATH FACES ONE OF THEM AND SAYS 'NOW I REPENT' NOR OF THOSE WHO DIE WHILE THEY ARE DISBELIEVERS" (Qur'an 4:18)

Muslims are urged to have faith in receiving rewards for their good deeds while being concerned about any sins they may commit. When they sin, they must be honest in their repentance and seek pardon of Allah. Finally, they are happy with the words of their creator and hold it dear to their hearts.

"SURELY ALLAH IS MOST GENTLE, EVER COMPASSIONATE TO PEOPLE" (Qur'an 22:65)

CHAPTER TWO

FAITH IN GOD

Faith is the acceptance of Allah, His angels, His revelations, His Prophets, the last day and the provision of all things, good or bad. Our dread of the unknown turns into faith when we realize that God loves us more than we can possibly imagine and that He always knows what is best for us. We experience more harmony in our lives as we place more trust in God's flawless wisdom. When we submit to God's will (even when things do not go according to our plan), we are grateful because we know that God's plan is always better than our wildest hopes. True liberation for the soul can only be attained by faith in His plan and submission to Allah. Allah calls us toward Him through unlimited mercy and love without any discrimination. He provides for the good, the bad and everything else that lies in between. In good and bad times, this existence is a test. As I am writing this, one story - the global pandemic brought on by the Corona Virus (CoVID 19) has been taking over the news cycle. It has emerged as a new strain of a fatal and contagious disease in recent years. This occurrence, which spread quickly across continents is undoubtedly a humble sign from Allah - The Almighty, who is able to cause such devastation with a microscopic organism that is undetectable to the naked eye. It is claiming lives and exhausting resources all at once. Many of the routine tasks we take for granted have come to a grinding halt as a result of the forced shutdown of businesses, schools and other institutions across the world. it still needs to be controlled. Pandemics do not make discriminations based on religion, nations, race, politics or social class. Allah endures despite the unpredictability, dread and sense of impending loss we experience as a result of these circumstances. God has promised ease in exchange for every affliction. Our faith assures us that this too shall pass but we must look for methods to sanctify ourselves and feed our spirits as we go through this test. The believer sees every opportunity as a chance to receive benefits and we continue to have faith in Allah-The Al-Merciful (Ar - Rahman) who never disappoints us and repeatedly leads us from darkness into light. Allah does not subject us to hardships without providing the resources to look for relief and facilitate our success. Beyond worldly worry and misery, the true test of difficulty is how we decide to react it. How do we overcome what seems to be out of our heads? How can we find meaning and comfort while overcoming our fears of the future, loneliness and the unknown?

"AND PUT THY TRUST IN ALLAH AND ENOUGH IS ALLAH AS A DISPOSER OF AFFAIRS"

The ability to have a cheerful attitude under any circumstance is one of a Muslim's key traits. He strives for excellence and seeks knowledge. A Muslim never loses hope, not even during the most difficult times. This is due to their belief that Allah is the creator of everything and that He has the ability to manifest anything He desires simply by saying it to "Be!"

The faithful understands that whatever difficult circumstances they encounter are a test from God. In keeping with what Allah has counselled him, he accepts things as they are remembering that "But perhaps you hate a thing and it is good for you; and perhaps you love a thing and it is bad for you. And Allah knows and you know not"(Qur'an 2:216). For a Muslim with such a deep soul, everything works well. Whatever the hardship or trouble, it is Allah who bestows it onto that person. he is the protector and helper of believers. Everything that Allah - The Almighty has made is for the best and is filled with knowledge.

The souls of believers who have a sincere and pure belief in Allah throughout this world's existence are taught by Allah to be deserving of Paradise. According to Allah's will, each step in this commandment allows Muslims to advance closer to Paradise. Making mistakes does not mean that one does not have faith. Humans are weak, fallible and defective creations of Allah. Muslims are humans like everyone else and make mistakes. But when Muslims become aware of the right path of action through their consciences or even if they do not but are reminded of it by others, they do not deliberately insist on continuing with their errors. It entails prompt repentance taking refuge in Allah and a determination to learn from one's mistakes rather than repeat them. This is a significant sign of a Muslim's sincerity. When Muslims act improperly, Allah instructs them how to respond: "Those who, recall Allah and ask forgiveness for their bad actions (and who can forgive bad actions but Allah) and do not knowingly continue doing what they were doing" (Qur'an, 3:135).

Muslims are valuable creators who carry the spirit of Allah. Such people should not magnify their errors and think worse of them as a result of them. Even before a person is born, it is already ordained in destiny at what time, on what date and where they will commit that error. Therefore, it is improper for people to lack confidence as a result of mistakes they have made. Muslims never pay heed to the approval of other people. They never dwell on questions like "I wander what people will say? How will they perceive me? Will they still adore me? Will I harm their faith in me?". Muslims just seek Allah's approval and blessings

Muslims are troubled by their consciences when they sin because they fear Allah. they start to think as the Qur'an instructs them and as a result, they recognize the truth. They, then experience regret for their sins, work to atone for them and uphold higher moral standards by turning to Allah for protection. They become more aware of how weak they are as a result of their mistakes. They come to a more profound realization of their dependence on Allah. This way of thinking improves one's humility and surrender to Allah.

CHAPTER THREE

GRATITUDE TOWARDS ALLAH

Giving praise to Allah and expressing thanks to Him are the acts of compassion. Due to the enormous favours and bounties that He has showered upon His slaves in both spiritual and material terms, Allah is the One who is most deserving of our gratitude and adoration. We are obligated by Allah to acknowledge and thank Him for all the gifts He has given us.

Practicing gratitude in Islam is the means to greater prosperity. we must be thankful for everything we have including our health, wealth, breath, friends, family and all other possessions. Most importantly, we must be grateful for being Muslims and members of the Ummah of Prophet (sallalahu aliahi wasalam). Allah appreciates people who give thanks to Him for everything they have. In addition to being the core and soul of Islam, Gratitude is the secret to bringing success, abundance and other positive traits into one's life. We can say that gratitude is the most significant facet of Islam. We should never stop being grateful to Allah for all his favours. He is One who created this planet and He is the most Merciful to all His people. If we express gratitude to Him, it indicates that we are believers. Allah - The Almighty states in the Holy Qur'an: "AND REMEMBER ! YOUR LORD CAUSED TO BE DECLARED : IF YOU ARE GRATEFUL, I WILL ADD MORE ONTO YOU" (Qur'an 14:5-7)

The road to loving Allah is gratitude(shukr). The only defence of shukr against unbelief is shukr. It serves as a remedy for sadness and materialism as well as inspiration for doing better the next day. giving someone a sincere "thank you" and "gratitude" is essentially returning the favour and praising them for their kind behaviour and thoughtfulness towards us. Moreover, we should always be grateful to Allah - The Almighty who is the kindest One. Allah commanded us to always endeavour to do shukr for what He has given us and to be thankful to Him for all of His benefits.

"THEREFORE REMEMBER ME (BY PRAYING, GLORIFYING). I WILL REMEMBER YOU AND BE GRATEFUL TO ME (FOR ,Y COUNTLESS FAVOURS ON YOU) AND NEVER BE UNGRATEFUL TO ME" (Qur'an 2:152)

Since Allah has endowed us with the capacity for gratitude, we ought to express our gratitude to the Almighty.

Benefits of Gratitude:

Gratitude fosters wellbeing and pleasure. Here are a few advantages of gratitude that we should be aware of so that anyone who is not yet giving thanks to Allah can begin doing Shukr:

1. *Better relationship with Allah:*

The finest approach to become nearer to Allah is to express gratitude. We request His pity and affection for us by means of Shukr. The path to Allah's reward and pleasure is via Allah's gratitude. When we express our gratitude to Him, we work to strengthen our bond with Allah - The Almighty.

"AND WHOEVER DESIRES TTHE REWARD OF THIS WORLD - WE WILL GIVE HIM THEREOF AND WHOEVER DESIRES THE REWARD OF THE HEREAFTER- WE WILL GIVE HIM THEREOF. AND WE WILL REWARD THE GRATEFUL" (Qur'an 3:145)

2. Success in Life:

Gratitude is a quality that will bring success in this life as wee as the hereafter. If we are thankful, Allah guarantees us kindness and an increase in His benefits.

"AND [REMEMBER] WHEN YOUR LORD PROCLAIMED 'IF YOU ARE GRATEFUL, I WILL SURELY INCREASE YOU [IN FAVOUR]'" (Qur'an 14:7)

From this verse, we can infer that if we are thankful to Allah for His blessings, he will shower us with numerous gifts in return.

3. Prevents Punishment of Allah:

When we thank Allah, He will bestow blessings upon us and He has every right to chastise us for our carelessness. Therefore, if we are grateful, he will bless us. Being thankful shields one from Allah's wrath.

4. Seeking pleasure of Allah:

Gratefulness is one of the most beautiful ways to please Allah both in this life and the hereafter. We spend out entire lives trying to please Allah. the finest way to bless ourselves with Allah's favour is through gratitude.

5. Reduce Materialism and increase sympathy:

The pursuit of true pleasure does not depend on material wealth. It has been demonstrated that gratitude actually lessens feelings of materialism and its detrimental impacts. Lower materialism and better life satisfaction are connected with greater displays of thankfulness. For leading a happy and contented life, we must be thankful to Allah.

Simple ways to show gratitude:

1. Contemplate His blessings in your life:

Understand and recognize that you must fulfil your obligations towards Allah. This is the primary way to be grateful and to show gratitude.

2. Be contented at Heart:

Instead of yearning for what others possess, we must learn to be contented with whatever we have while avoiding exhausting ourselves and stepping on someone else in the process. We would not find peace of mind if we are continually comparing our financial situations or sense of wellbeing to that of others. There can be no happiness of heart without mental tranquillity. So, instead of feeling jealous when you see someone living a life of luxury or succeeding in life, just be happy for them. Give your best and keep in mind that the will of Allah governs all that happens to you.

3. Remain committed in times of ease:

When things are going well, it is simple to think that nothing can grow wrong. As a result, it is possible to forget to remember Allah and get caught up in everyday life. We frequently make promises to change ourselves in order to avoid a particular trial but as soon as we are spared from it, we resume our immoral behaviour. It is crucial to continue to be grateful to Allah and mindful of His precepts, not simply when it is convenient to do so.

4. Be Patient in Difficult times:

What is the better approach to overcome a challenge than to demonstrate patience? instead of feeling defeated, have faith that Allah will guide you through the finish line.

"INDEED NO ONE DESPAIRS OF RELIEF FROM ALLAH EXCEPT THE DISBELIEVING PEOPLE" (Qur'an 12:87)

We may grow and learn from the challenge we face as long as we keep in mind that they do not continue forever. Being impatient when things are difficult is a sign of frail faith and narrow mindedness. It merely increases frustration rather than doing anything to lessen the misery.

5. Do not waste your Blessings:

Waste of food, water and other resources is a demonstration of disregard for Allah's favour. While eating, the Prophet (sallalahu alaihi wasalam) used to exhort people to clean the dish and not leave any food particle behind (Abu Dawud). around the world, millions of people lack access to necessities like regular meals and clean water. therefore, every meal that ends up in a trash, rather be given to someone in need, is contributing to eliminating hunger and poverty. On the other hand, by appreciating the gifts ones has and reducing waste, one may ensure a more equitable allocation of resources while also showing gratitude.

6. Share your blessings with others:

Allah is the ultimate owner of everything. We are merely the temporary beneficiaries. We should share our blessings with fellow humans. Helping those in need is described by Allah as giving Him a loan that He will repay many times over (Qur'an 2:245). Our level of thankfulness will increase the more we share with others we love. We should make sure that neither greed nor apathy prevents us from giving selflessly.

7. Value your relationships:

Be grateful for the people in your environment who enrich your life. Consider the favours that each significant person in your life has shown you. Do not take anything for granted including your friends, parents, spouse, kids or anyone else. Never let a conflict or negative interaction with one person affect how you act towards others. Consider ways to strengthen your bonds with others while keeping in mind that Allah is the one who has placed you in their company.

8. Obey the commands of Allah:

The most practical form of gratitude is obedience to the commands of Allah. You acknowledge Allah's superiority over you and His numerous benefits upon you by obeying Him. Make every effort to encourage what is right and forbid what is wrong. Even if the truth contradicts you, keep fighting for it. Moreover, putting your own desires ahead of Allah's instructions is utterly unappreciative and hinders your spiritual development.

9. Thank people who show you kindness:

anytime someone does something for you, no matter how tiny, let them know that you appreciate it. Never consider any act of kindness as insignificant and make it a point to thank the person who is supporting you. As the Prophet (sallalahu alaihi wasalam) said, "He who does not thank people is not thankful to Allah". Thank the person who holds the door open for you, helps you at the store or calls just to have a polite conversation.

10. Express Gratitude with words:

Every day, call upon Allah to thank Him for His infinite blessings. Start each day's prayer of gratitude with the words,

"O Allah, I am thankful to you for providing me all these benefits" and the list as many of them as you can. Alternatively, think about one blessing for which you are grateful every day. Every time, you eat or drink something or anytime something wonderful happens to you, thank Allah by saying "Alhamdulillah". Recall Allah often, address Him directly and be thankful to Him for His kindness and generosity.

CHAPTER FOUR

DHIKR - REMEMBRANCE OF ALLAH

In Islam, the word 'Dhikr' means remembrance and in the Islamic context, it is used in the sense of remembrance of Allah.

"O YOU WHO BELIEVE! REMEMBER ALLAH WITH MUCH REMEMBRANCE." (QUR'AN 33:41)

Dhikr is a broad phrase that encompasses a variety of actions of the tongue and heart in addition to the formal acts of worship. It entails remembering and mentioning Allah constantly and in every facet of our existence. This type of worship is continuous and takes place at no particular time, permanently connecting a person's life to Allah and His service.

"THEN REMEMBER ME, I WILL REMEMBER YOU."
(QUR'AN 2:152)

There are other more ways to remember Allah in addition to our traditional acts of worship, such as salat - prayer, which is the one we perform most frequently. The most important of these is reading and reciting the Quran. At least 55 different times in the Quran, Allah has mentioned "Adh-dhikr," which is Arabic for "The Remembrance" or "The Reminder. The most efficient way to remember Allah is to read, comprehend, think, and analyse His words.

Dhikr also entails remembering Allah when one wakes up in the morning, before beginning any activity, while eating, when leaving the house, when entering other locations, and before carrying out a plethora of other tasks. All of our efforts add up to His memory and worship if we can recite the right prayers for each occasion as our Prophet (PBUH) advised us to do. These can be learned with a little effort, but if for some reason one is unable to recall the proper one, then simply the simple act of saying "Bismillah" and being aware of Allah counts as dhikr and will bring blessings to all our actions (barakah).

Remembering Allah simply refers to adoration, love, and worship of Allah in order to give thanks and therefore become the thankful servants of our Creator. Remembering Allah is the best method to express your sincere thankfulness to Him for His protection and innumerable blessings. The ultimate goal of all forms of worship is to remember Allah with focus and presence of mind. A dhakir (one who recite dhikr and is engaged in the recollection of Allah) will attain a rank where the Devil will be unable to defeat and subdue him if he is focused on Allah in his heart and acts. Dhikr, or remembering Allah, consists of two fundamental concepts: how your tongue moves and how that affects your heart. It should be felt deeply in your heart as much as in the movement of your tongue. Of course, simply saying "Subhan Allah" and "Alhamdulillah" is a blessing in and of itself. However, you can only fully experience Allah and His religion's holiness and love when you immerse yourself in His Dhikr.

Dhikr includes reciting the Quran, being kind to others and speaking good of others in a broader sense. This teaches us that Dhikr can be any good deed performed with the right intention. Allah mentions in verse 181 of Surah Al - Imran:

"WHO REMEMBERS ALLAH WHILE STANDING OR SITTING OR (LYING) ON THEIR SIDES AND GIVE THOUGHT TO THE CREATION OF THE HEAVENS AND THE EARTH, (SAYING), 'OUR LORD, YOU DID NOT CREATE THIS AIMLESSLY; EXALTED

ARE YOU (ABOVE SUCH A THING); THEN PROTECT US FROM THE PUNISHMENT OF THE FIRE'".

Indeed, if Allah has mentioned those who engage in Dhikr, then He has truly bestowed uncountable and unimaginable rewards on them. Dhikr can be performed anywhere, anytime, unlike salah, which must be performed at specific times and in a pure environment. It can be done by thinking thoughts of Allah in one's heart or by repeating specific formulations to glorify and praise Allah.

Who among us has experienced times when life overwhelms us and it is difficult to maintain our ibadah and remembrance of Allah? The first person to put up their hand is me! However, since Allah should come first in whatever we do, there really shouldn't be a justification for this. It can occasionally feel overwhelming with everything you have to do—working, travelling, chores, caring for your family, and a million other things. As odd as it may sound, we frequently feel busier than ever despite the fact that technology is meant to make things more effective and time-saving. Here, i am describing some of the ways to increase Dhikr:

1. Use technology to its fullest potential to learn useful information:

Use this time to learn something new about the Deen or to review what you already know, as opposed to turning on the radio as soon as you get in the car, checking social media as you wait for your train, or watching TV while doing chores. There are numerous Quran recitation applications as well as YouTube video lecture series and podcasts where you may locate your favourite speakers on a variety of themes. Take some time to put together your playlist for your commute or downtimes by choosing a speaker or subject that interests you. How much you can genuinely learn while travelling will amaze you. Mu'awiyah (May Allah be pleased with him) reported:

"When Allah wishes good for someone, He bestows upon him the understanding of Deen," [Muslim and Al-Bukhari].

2. Read a verse from the Qur'an every day:

Build a slow and steady engagement with the Qur'an by beginning to incorporate it into your daily life. At the absolute least, try reciting one verse a day, thinking about it and applying its lessons to your life when you can.The Prophet (pbuh) said: "Whoever reads one letter from the Book of Allah will get one reward by doing so," according to Abdullah Ibn Masud's narration. Ten prizes of comparable kind are equal to one reward. Alif is a letter, Lam is a letter, and Meem is a letter—not that Alif-Lam-Meem is a letter. [Tirmidhi]. If you believe that you do not recite the Qur'an very well, don't worry. Everyone starts somewhere, and it is so worth the effort! Aishah (May Allah be pleased with her) reported:

"The one who is skilled in the recitation of the Qur'an will be with the honourable and obedient scribes (angels) and he who recites the Qur'an but finds it difficult, doing his best to recite it in the best way possible, will have a double reward," said the Messenger of Allah. [Muslims and Al-Bukhari]. Can you picture receiving additional rewards simply because we have difficulty reciting the Qur'an?

3. Strive to maintain ablution at all times:

Being in a continuous state of ablution (wudu) serves to keep us mindful of Allah's memory. Additionally, by doing it this way, you can conduct your salah whenever you want and will also get many benefits. The Messenger of Allah (may Allah be pleased with him) reportedly said," Should I not direct you to that by which Allah erases the sins and raises (your) ranks? They said, "Yes, O Messenger of Allah," He said, "Performing Wudu' correctly, even when it is difficult, regularly visiting the mosque, and anxiously anticipating the subsequent Salat (prayer) when a Salat is over; truly, it is Ar- Ribat," [Muslim]. Performing wudu not only earns us the reward, but it also keeps us clean and fresh all day long.

4. Structure your day around your prayers:

Have you ever been in a hurry to perform your salah because the time is almost up? We have all probably experienced this before. In contrast, things seem to move more smoothly and you actually feel like you have more time to accomplish other tasks when you are truly praying as the time for prayer begins. Abdullah (may Allah have mercy on him) narrated: "Which act is the most precious to Allah", I asked the Prophet (PBUH)? "To say the prayers at their early, designated regular times" he (PBUH) responded. [Bukhari]. Planning your day around your required prayers has a tonne of advantages; After all, the adhan says" Haiya 'Alas-salah, Haiya 'Alal-falah" (Come to prayer, Come to success). It certainly helps if you are already constantly in wudu. Everything else will be simple for you once you have finished with your most crucial task for the day. Watch how this tip changes your hectic day!

5. Engage in mindfulness:

Being mindful in your regular activities can improve your relationship with Allah in significant ways. Try to be sincere and renew your intentions in all you do for Allah's sake. We would not only be more aware of what we do but because Allah is the Most Generous, we would also be rewarded for the ordinary things we perform every day. Who here hasn't been distracted by the ding of a notification on their phone or had their attention stray to a billion other things when engaged in prayer? This is one of the most crucial times of the day to be especially alert. Being attentive of Allah even before entering the prayer space will help you focus and be more present during your prayers. Put your phone on aeroplane mode for the 10 to 15 minutes that you spend praying and keep in mind that you are standing in front of Allah (glorified and exalted be He) when you are praying.

6. Choose a few duas or dhikr to concentrate on:

Perhaps you don't often make dhikr or duas but this is the perfect moment to start. Maximize your downtime by reciting some dhikr, such as the morning and evening remembrances or any other duas, whether you are waiting to board a flight, doing the dishes, delayed in traffic while commuting to work or just have a few minutes to spare before your day gets underway. To properly understand the meaning of what you are saying, start small and choose just a few that speak to you personally. Then, gradually increase from there. The comprehensive "anti-procrastination dua," which is an excellent way to start the day is one of my favourite duas that I'm attempting to remember by heart:

"Allahumma inni 'a'udhubika minal hammi walhuzni, Wal'ajzi walkasali, walbukhli waljubni, Wa dal'id-daiyni wa ghalabatir-rajal."

'O Allah, I take refuge in You from anxiety and sorrow, weakness and laziness, miserliness and cowardice, the burden of debts and from being over powered by men.' [Bukhari] Dua is not merely to be made following prayer. Dua can be made anytime, anywhere and in any language you understand. Dua also includes silently praying in your heart. Become accustomed to speaking with Allah. After all, He declares in Surah Ghafir, "Call upon Me, and I will respond to you." (40:60)

7. Give Charity:

Sadaqah (voluntary acts of charity) are not limited to monetary donations. There is a lovely hadith that states: "Your smile to your brother is a sadaqah (charitable act) for you," the Prophet of Allah (PBUH) is quoted as saying by Abu Dhar. A sadaqah is when you perform the right and forbid the bad. A sadaqah for you is guiding a guy in the area of misguidance. Your sadaqah is to see (see the way) for a man with poor vision. It is a sadaqah for you when you remove a stone, thorn or bone from the road. Your sadaqah is to empty your bucket of water into your brother's (empty) bucket. [Tirmidhi]. Isn't that incredible? Almost anything you do for someone else, no matter how great or small, counts as an act of charity if it is done for Allah's sake. Find a daily habit that speaks to you personally and is simple for you to practise, even if it is as simple as holding open the door for someone or offering one compliment per day. Setting up a monthly auto-debit with any of your chosen charities or organisations is another simple method to guarantee that you always get the benefits of doing good.

8. Spend time with positive people:

Whether it is in real life or merely online, we're all social creatures. It has a great effect to be around people who are conscious of Allah and endeavour to do good. For instance, if praying five times a day is challenging for you, find a friend who practises it and go to your prayers with them. When we surround ourselves with people who also remember Allah, it is simpler to do so. The people we follow online also have an impact on how we view the world. It is crucial for us to select and choose who we follow online and utilise social media for the good of others because it is quite easy to become engrossed in the lives of those behind the screen.

9. Give greetings of peace:

Have you ever exchanged greetings of peace with a fellow Muslim while travelling in a strange nation and grinned ear to ear? Something about communicating those messages of peace to one another fosters relationships and cheers the spirit. Did you know that one of the most potent means of entering paradise is something as simple as offering greetings to someone else? Abdullah bin Salam (May Allah be pleased with him) reported:

I heard the Messenger of Allah (ﷺ) saying, "O people, exchange greetings of peace (i.e., say: As-Salamu 'Alaikum to one another), feed people, strengthen the ties of kinship and be in prayer when others are asleep, you will enter Jannah in peace." [At-Tirmidhi]

No matter where you are in the universe, don't forget to perform this incredibly basic act, especially to keep your ties to your community strong.

10. Practice Gratitude every day:

It goes without saying that those who are grateful tend to be happier people. Even recent Western research supports this! Simply take a look at any self-help book, and you'll see that one of its main principles is to keep a gratitude list or something similar. That Allah has previously informed us of this in the Qur'an, which was revealed more than 1400 years ago, is wonderful, isn't it?

AND KEEP IN MIND WHAT YOUR LORD SAID: "IF YOU ARE GRATEFUL, I WILL SURELY INCREASE YOU [IN FAVOUR]; BUT IF YOU DENY, INDEED, MY PUNISHMENT IS SEVERE." [Qur'an 14:7]

You will see that Allah does actually give more in response to the duas made by the Prophets in the Qur'an (who are, of course, the best models of practising patience and thankfulness). For instance, the Prophet Zakariya (peace be upon him) prayed for a son even though his wife was infertile and he was old. In addition to giving them a son, Allah also made the Prophet Yahya (peace be upon him) their son!

From the oxygen we breathe to the roof over our heads, there is always something for which to be thankful. Being mindful of everything Allah has provided for us would undoubtedly make us feel closer to Him.

www.ingramcontent.com/pod-product-compliance
Lightning Source LLC
Chambersburg PA
CBHW021157130726
47988CB00004B/1656